The El Paso Chile Company

*Dear Mom —
I love you
very much!
This fun book
reminds me of your
fabulous
entertaining skills
S. Celia*

Viva Vodka

Colorful Cocktails
with a Kick

by W. Park Kerr

Photographs
by Leigh Beisch

CHRONICLE BOOKS
SAN FRANCISCO

Library of Congress
Cataloging-in-Publication Data available.

ISBN-10: 0-8118-5176-1

ISBN-13: 978-0-8118-5176-3

Manufactured in China.

Prop styling by Sara Slavin
Food styling by Dan Becker
Designed by Michael Mabry Design

Distributed in Canada by
Raincoast Books
9050 Shaughnessy Street
Vancouver, British Columbia V6P 6E5

10 9 8 7 6 5 4 3 2 1

Chronicle Books LLC
85 Second Street
San Francisco, California 94105

www.chroniclebooks.com

Dedication

To my pals: Chris Hill and Rodolfo "Chope" Choperena . . .
two of the best global vodka-swilling buddies on the planet.
The Arrivederci Capri is inspired by the most delicious sum-
mers with you guys, my family, old and new friends at Casa
Moneta, sipping homemade lemoncello, smuggled vodka,
and the long climb home from the Bar Tiberio . . . this one is
for you. Multo Graci. —WPK

Acknowledgments

Once again, hats and bottle tops off to Mittie Hellmich,
mistress mixologist and killer co-author. M3, your uncanny
ability to mix up the perfectly shaken, stirred, or burred
libation is delicious. San Francisco photo team of master-
shooter Leigh Beisch, the rockin' food styling of Dan Becker,
the dishy Sara Slavin, and Angelica Arriaga Cao. And to our
four-legged pals Bella and Kikka. Brilliant Emeryville book
designers Michael Mabry and Peter Soe Jr. The crew at
Chronicle Books, especially, once again, Bill LeBlond, who
is the kind of editor and guy that inspires the best and most
creative work out of his favorite author. Bill, you are always
perfectly chilled but never shaken!

Contents

Vodka is wonderfully polymorphous—it becomes whatever you want it to be—and we love that!

A cocktail lover's dream, vodka is so versatile that it mixes swimmingly with just about any ingredient your palate desires. With its clean, pure, tasteless character, this chameleonlike spirit can also be a bit dangerous; after a few delectable Lemon Drops or Chocolatinis, you may not be quite sure what hit you.

Renowned for taking the chill off northern European winters by way of viscous, frosty shots, vodka conjures impressions that are romantically inseparable from mother Russia. But today's vodka aficionados also pay tribute to Poland and Scandinavia, where fine-quality vodkas have been produced for centuries, as well as to the premium brands produced in France and the United States. Before you get seduced into shaking all the delicious multinectared concoctions in this book and beyond, we encourage you to learn to fully appreciate vodka by experiencing a few super-premiums sip by sip. We diligently taste-tested quite a few and offer in the beginning of the book a list of our favorite best-quality vodkas to guide you as you explore whether you prefer a creamy potato-based vodka from Poland, a subtle citrus-flavored vodka from France, or a clean, astringent vodka from Sweden.

This purest of spirits has come a long way, baby, from its early melancholic associations as the fortifier for downtrodden Russian writers and Communist revolutionaries to the current liquid darling of contemporary cocktails. Vodka was virtually unknown outside Russia, Poland, and Scandinavia until "from Russia with love" came Vladimir Smirnoff, who brought it to the west in the 1930s, thus beginning vodka's evolution into the fabric of America's culture. In the swinging sixties, it was the extremely popular James Bond, with his storied preference for Russian vodka, who was the catalyst for a macho chic trend of drinking Vodka Martinis, bringing a hip legitimacy to the spirit as a swank and stylish alternative to the traditional gin. But vodka's winning attribute of pure, neutral taste came into full mixological play in the 1970s, when it became the chosen spirit for a variety of deceivingly coy cocktails, bringing on those liqueur-heavy girly drinks and shooters with the erotic names that hid their alcoholic velocity in a creamy sweetness.

In *Viva Vodka* we represent the best of vodka's sixties suave and seventies spike, but our exploration with vodka doesn't stop there. Flavored vodkas open up a whole other realm of flavor possibilities. Although an ancient practice, infusing spirits with herbal and other ingredients has enjoyed a thorough resurgence in popularity and has become the hottest ticket to innovation in contemporary cocktails. Vodka infusions, from rosemary to mango to quadruple-citrus, are a great way to expand your Martini repertoire and add subtle excitement to any number of cocktails. Steeping your favorite fruit, herb, or spice is so easy, there's no excuse for not having a few creative vodka concoctions chilling in the refrigerator, in anticipation of treating your guests to a sublime vodka experience.

We hope that you enjoy this little book full of fabulously creative concoctions inspired by classic drinks, new classics, and all the luscious ingredients that take so well with vodka. In the pages ahead you'll find how-tos for homemade infusions and gorgeous, edible rims, and over 95 recipes for elegant cocktails, shooters from the simple to the spectacular, refreshing patio coolers, frozen and creamy indulgences, and dazzling new combinations, all beckoning you for some serious shaking.

Za vashe zdorovye!

Vodka 101

Vodka means "little water" in Russian, and the name fittingly captures the characteristics of this clean, clear spirit, which was traditionally made to have as little discernible flavor or aroma as possible. The origins of the first vodkas can be traced back to the twelfth century, in northeastern Europe. These early distillations were harsh and oily, and were in fact initially used as a cleaning astringent for the skin. But the product soon evolved into a drinkable spirit that many of that time period used as a balm with which to escape the woes of a bleak and hard life.

Today there is a wide selection of premium and super-premium vodkas available worldwide that go beyond anything imagined in the twelfth century. Originally made mostly in Poland, Russia, and Scandinavia, vodka didn't show up on American shores until around 1939, when Vladimir Smirnoff exported his distilling expertise. Even then, vodka didn't really begin to take off until the Moscow Mule was introduced in the mid-1940s, a promotional drink invented specifically to sell the unfamiliar and seemingly exotic Russian spirit. Word spread, and by the 1960s, America was so completely enamored of vodka, with its distinctively neutral taste and versatility, that it had become the number one seller in the liquor market.

Vodka Creation

For all the hype and posturing evoking a mysterious and complex process for making vodka—organic grains or potatoes, elaborate filtration through quartz or limestone, numerous distillations, the purest of glacial waters—it is actually quite a simple process.

A mash of rye, wheat, or potatoes is fermented and then distilled, typically in a continuous still, a modernized and efficient way to produce larger volumes and a purer product.

A few distillers choose to use the traditional pot still method; relatively more old-world and rudimentary, it lends itself to producing vodkas with a slightly more flavorful quality. Many vodkas are distilled four or more times to achieve a clean spirit. Lastly, the distillate is filtered to remove any of the remaining congeners (flavoring compounds) that would normally impart flavors and aromas. Unlike other spirits, there is no addition of botanicals during distillation or aging time in barrels, methods that typically add flavor. The simplicity of the process is reflected in the resulting pure, clean, neutral qualities of vodka; its mild smoothness is achieved through multiple filtrations rather than by aging.

Historically vodka was made with whatever grains were available, such as rye, wheat, corn, or barley, and in nineteenth-century Poland, potatoes. Technically, vodka can be made from just about any substance, from molasses to sugar beets to millet or even from grapes, as with the ultra-stylish grape-based Ciroc vodka from France. Once distilled and specially filtered, usually through activated charcoal (the highest-quality vodkas are filtered many times) the resulting spirit is rendered neutral in aroma, taste, and color. The distinctions between brands are, however, due in part to the substance from which they are made, especially the premium vodkas, which strive to retain a whisper of the original elements to impart a discernible personality into the spirit. Potatoes characteristically produce vodka with a creamy quality, whereas grain-based vodkas tend to be smooth and fruity, with rye-based vodkas having a bite and wheat a more subtle delicacy.

With a virtual absence of flavor, how it feels on the palate is the most prominent feature of vodka. Qualities such as oily, soft, viscous, or buttery add up to what is called the "mouth-feel" of the spirit. However, many of the super-premium vodkas that are in such demand these days also tout a wide range of subtly detected botanical flavors, rendering this spirit that has traditionally been by definition a blank canvas ironically flavorful.

When it comes to categorizing the multitude of vodka styles, generally speaking, the country of origin is a good divining rod. Western vodkas are, for the most part, dependable but unremarkable and well suited for cocktail mixing, whereas Eastern European distillers, who continue to produce the most highly esteemed vodkas, offer spirits with an emphasis on a pleasing uniqueness in mouthfeel, smoothness, and subtle but discernible flavors.

Vodka is inseparable from Russian culture, conjuring Dostoyevskian images of frosty shots chased with strong black bread. From Smirnoff to Stolichnaya, the Russians' reputation for making elegant, clean spirits is holding steady. Stolichnaya, one of the most popular Russian vodkas, is a wheat-based vodka, offered in both a moderately priced and a premium style. The regular "Stoli" is oily in body, silky smooth, and slightly fragrant. The premium, Stoli Gold, is extremely smooth and slightly peppery, with a thick, syrupy mouthfeel.

Although Poland's vodka is historically linked to the potato, most of the Polish vodkas currently available are made from grain. Happily, there are a few potato-based vodkas of superior quality still made: look for Chopin, Luksusowa, and Quotes. Holland puts out one of today's most elegant-tasting vodkas, Ketel One, which is distilled by the traditional pot still method. One of the most popular brands of vodka in the world, Absolut, is produced in Sweden, with a taste that has been described as clean and light with a whisper of lemon and pine notes. Finland is known for its state-of-the-art distilleries, and produces, of course, Finlandia vodka, a pure, light, citrusy spirit; Finlandia also makes a great cranberry-flavored vodka ideal for using in a Cosmopolitan.

Although general consensus on vodka is that the farther north it hails from, the better it is, there are always exceptions. France, for example, produces a few outstanding premium vodkas, among them Citadelle and Grey Goose. America also produces a few great premium vodkas, such as Skyy and Rain, which exhibit nuances of flavor; the quintessential example of the American style of vodka making, however, is American-produced Smirnoff, which is very clean, with absolutely no trace of flavor.

When choosing a top-shelf vodka, either for Martinis, sipping or those traditional vodka shots, you want the highest-quality super-premium you can find to best enjoy its subtleties in those straightforward libations. Don't waste these in a Cosmo or Bloody Mary; the super-premium vodkas will just get lost in all the other flavors, and it's not worth the expense. For mixed drinks, pick up a good-quality vodka such as moderately priced Smirnoff, or kick it up with a premium vodka such as Absolut, Skyy, or Stolichnaya, all dependably good vodkas at reasonable prices.

Our Picks for the Best Super-Premium Vodkas

You can generally divide vodka drinkers into two camps: those vodka aficionados who enjoy exploring the subtle taste differences in the spectrum of vodkas and those who insist that the perceived differences and nuances between brands are practically indiscernible, and that just about any type of vodka, once chilled in the freezer, will make a fine Vodka Martini. With that in mind, here is our purely subjective list of recommended high-end super-premium vodkas, complete with flowery adjectives describing their flavors and aromas, real or imagined. Ultimately, the choice always comes down to personal preference, and you may even find yourself equally seduced by the hip and stylish bottle designs as well.

- Belvedere, from Poland, is one of the most popular and consistently high-ranking super-premiums. Made from rye and charcoal filtered four times, for a smooth, subtle, and refined vodka with a hint of botanicals, vaguely astringent and peppery.

- Chopin is a great Polish vodka made from potatoes, quadruple-distilled for an odorless but rich, buttery feel; super-smooth with citrus tones and no discernible aftertaste.

- Citadelle, from France, is wheat based, with anise and black-currant aromas.

- Grey Goose is an aromatic vodka from France with purported flavors from vanilla to berries, pine to pear, and even chocolate.

- Ketel One, a wheat-based vodka from Holland, is another popular favorite. Smooth and creamy with sea spray and floral tones.

- Luksusowa, from Poland, is one of the best potato vodkas, with a verdant aroma, a hint of vanilla, and a viscous sweetness.

- Quotes, from Poland, is another deluxe triple-distilled potato vodka, slightly aromatic.

- Rain, a small-batch American vodka, is made from organic white corn. Clean and delicate, extremely smooth and soft.

- Skyy, from America, is made from grain. Crisp with hints of pepper and nuttiness.

- Wyborowa, a rye vodka from Poland, has hints of lime, is exceptionally smooth, and is one of the best overall examples of Polish vodka. A huge perk with this vodka is the fabulous bottle, which was designed by architect Frank Gehry.

Sipping Vodka

Most Americans prefer their vodka mixed in cocktails, with the exception of Vodka Martini fans, but the Russians, Poles, Swedes, and Western Europeans mainly still enjoy their vodka neat. If you want to enjoy the European vodka-sipping experience—whether straight in a shot glass, Moscow-style, or shaken and strained into a Martini glass—the super-premium vodkas are the only choice; for the most part, the super-premiums are indeed discernibly better in both smoothness and mouthfeel, ideal for sipping straight.

Anything of lesser quality tends to have a somewhat harsh finish and is really only suitable for mixed drinks.

The traditional European ritual of serving vodka straight from the freezer enhances its characteristic viscosity, giving it an enjoyable syrupy texture, and some vodka-lovers believe this also enhances the flavor. One school of connoisseurs insists vodka be at room temperature to fully experience all the ultra-subtle flavors, but usually it is served ice-cold and neat in a small, chilled-to-frostiness glass, to be savored in one gulp. Others enjoy straight vodka over ice, but purists find it sacrilegious to dilute premium vodka.

Of course, taste-testing different super-premiums is a fabulous way to navigate your way to a favorite. To help discern the multiple, complex dimensions of the best spirits, pay attention to the smell, flavor nuances, burn (whether aggressive or smooth—the best have a lack of bite), and aftertaste (from nonexistent and clean to too medicinal), as well as the mouthfeel (whether oily, syrupy, silky, or velvety).

For the quintessential vodka-sipping experience, always have on hand some finger food such as caviar, dark rye bread, dill pickles, and whitefish (herring) or oysters, with a mineral water chaser. Then, not only are you experiencing the time-honored way to enjoy your chilled shots of super-premium vodka, but the food will help you stay aware of how many shots you've had.

Finally, be sure to clink glasses and toast *Na zdorovial* (To your health) before sipping!

Flavored Vodkas

Although it may seem like a trendy contemporary concept, the use of herbs, spices, and fruits to flavor vodka is actually an age-old practice of many a Polish and Russian household.

With all the innovative mixology going on, flavored vodkas have exploded on the market in an ever-widening variety of choices. These days you can easily find flavors beyond the usual lemon or orange. From grapefruit, peach, and chocolate to black currant, apple, pepper, cranberry, mandarin, and vanilla, they open up a whole new world of creative cocktail options.

While flavored vodkas are now readily available on the shelves, there is nothing like homemade infused vodkas. Easy to throw together, with infinite possibilities, they are a superior option when you're ready for your next vodka cocktail experience. Following are our suggestions for luscious flavor combinations and how to make them.

Vodka Infusions

Infused liquors are the new medium for creative expression in the realm of cocktail mixology, and vodka is the ideal spirit for experimentation, as any number of ingredients easily infuse into this neutral-tasting liquor and shine through with clarity.

Beyond the basic citrus infusions, you can even take the concept to the next level of creativity by using, for example, a combination of tropical fruits, or adding fiery bite with hot peppers. Subtle herb infusions perfect for exotic vodka martinis are obtainable with just a sprig or two of rosemary or basil. Infusions are surprisingly easy to make, with an end result of wonderful depth of flavor. These are exceptional when served chilled and neat, and are handy for quick cocktails with nuance and complexity.

Basic Infusion Guidelines

1. Use a clean, large (at least 1.5-liter) glass container with an airtight lid for your infusion.

2. Start with a 750-ml bottle of good-quality vodka, and use fresh spices, herbs, or ripe fruit; the average yield will be about 3 cups.

3. Save your original bottle; you will need it to strain the infused mixture into.

4. Infusion times vary depending on the ingredient. Strong flavors like lemon take less time to steep (24 to 48 hours), while milder flavors such as raspberry or pineapple may take 1 to 2 weeks to fully infuse.

5. Some ingredients may break down as they stand, requiring the infusion to be strained through a wire-mesh strainer lined with a coffee filter or cheesecloth.

6. Infusions are best stored in the refrigerator; chilling helps preserve the flavors longer than if kept at room temperature.

Clove Vodka

This spicy, warming infusion adds an exotic edge to cocktails and is especially great when served shaken and chilled in a Martini.

25 whole cloves
One 750-ml bottle good-quality vodka

Place the cloves in a large glass container, add the vodka and cap tightly. Let stand at room temperature for 24 hours, shaking gently occasionally. Taste for the preferred flavor intensity, allowing it to infuse for another day if needed. (Do not allow it to infuse any longer than 2 weeks or a bitter flavor will result.) Strain the infused vodka into the original bottle. Cap tightly, label, and refrigerate until ready to serve.

Green Apple-Clove Vodka

This tart and spicy infusion adds a puckery edge to cocktails and is especially great when used in Apple Martinis (page 73).

2 Granny Smith apples, sliced
½ Gala apple, sliced
25 whole cloves
One 750-ml bottle good-quality vodka

Place the apple slices and cloves in a large glass container, add the vodka, and cap tightly. Let stand at room temperature for 1 week, shaking gently every couple of days. Taste for the preferred flavor intensity, allowing it to infuse for up to another week if needed. (Do not allow it to infuse any longer than 2 weeks or a bitter flavor will result.) Strain the infused vodka into the original bottle. Cap tightly, label, and refrigerate until ready to serve.

Coconut Vodka

This infusion is great for tropical-inspired cocktails, including the Pravda Colada (page 125).

Look for furry brown "easy crack" coconuts that are scored around the center and sound like they have liquid sloshing around inside when shaken; the three dark spots (or eyes) should be dry. If you don't want to go to the trouble of cracking open the nut to get to the fresh, crisp coconut meat inside, you can use prepared shredded fresh coconut, but the resulting flavor of your infusion will be more subtle.

3 cups freshly grated coconut (about 3 coconuts)
One 750-ml bottle good-quality vodka

With an ice pick, or other pointed sharp instrument, pierce the eyes and drain the coconut water into a glass. Crack open the shell by tapping a hammer along the scored line, or wrap it in a towel and whack it a few times. Cut the white flesh out with a knife and then grate the coconut meat with a handheld grater.

Place the coconut in a large glass container, add the vodka, and cap tightly. Let stand at room temperature for 3 weeks, shaking gently every couple of days. Taste for the preferred flavor intensity, allowing it to infuse for up to another week if needed. Strain the infused vodka into the original bottle. Cap tightly, label, and refrigerate until ready to serve.

Coffee Vodka

This infusion is perfect for Espresso Martinis (page 82).

20 coffee beans
One 750-ml bottle good-quality vodka

Place the coffee beans in a large glass container, add the vodka and cap tightly. Let stand at room temperature for 24 hours, shaking gently occasionally. Taste for the preferred flavor intensity, allowing it to infuse for another day if needed. (Do not allow it to infuse any longer than 2 weeks or a bitter flavor will result.) Strain the infused vodka into the original bottle. Cap, label, and refrigerate until ready to serve.

Lavender Vodka

This vodka infusion has a delicate, fragrant flavor that is key to a fabulous Lavender Martini. You can also substitute ½ cup fresh rosemary sprigs, 2 cups of fresh mint leaves, 1 cup fresh orange blossom petals, 1 cup fresh violet petals, or 1 cup fresh rose petals for the lavender. Infusion times will vary depending on the flower petal, so taste-test every day or so. Fresh petals are preferable, but if they are unavailable, you can use dried flower petals found at most natural-food stores; use ¼ cup dried flowers for a 750-ml bottle of vodka.

¼ cup fresh lavender
1 small piece vanilla bean (optional)
One 750-ml bottle good-quality vodka

Place the lavender and vanilla bean, if using, in a large glass container, add the vodka, and cap tightly. Let stand at room temperature for 2½ to 3 weeks, shaking gently every 3 or 4 days. Taste for the preferred flavor intensity, allowing it to infuse for another day or two if needed. (Do not allow it to infuse any longer than 3½ weeks or a bitter flavor will result.) Strain the infused vodka into the original bottle. Cap tightly, label, and refrigerate until ready to serve.

Vanilla Vodka

This is one of the most popular and versatile infusions, adding a warm spicy dimension to many vodka cocktails, especially the Chocolatini (page 79).

3 to 4 vanilla beans, broken into small pieces
One 750-ml bottle good-quality vodka

Add the vanilla bean pieces to the bottle of vodka and cap tightly. Let stand for at least 1 week, shaking gently every couple of days. Leave the vanilla in the bottle to infuse indefinitely and refrigerate. When ready to use, slowly strain the vanilla-infused vodka through a fine-mesh wire strainer into the jigger or glass.

Kumquat-Vanilla Vodka

When you pair tart kumquats, a grape-sized orange citrus fruit, with vanilla bean, the result is a lushly aromatic and zesty combination that adds an exciting exotic flavor dimension to vodka coolers and Martinis alike.

16 kumquats, sliced in half
2 vanilla beans, broken into small pieces
One 750-ml bottle good-quality vodka

Place the kumquats and vanilla bean pieces in a large glass container, add the vodka, and cap tightly. Let stand at room temperature for 1 week, shaking gently every couple of days. Taste for the preferred flavor intensity, allowing it to infuse for up to another week if needed. (Do not allow it to infuse any longer than 2 weeks, or a bitter flavor will result.) Strain the infused vodka into the original bottle (you can leave the vanilla in the bottle to infuse indefinitely if you wish). Cap tightly, label, and refrigerate until ready to serve.

Ginger Vodka

This Pan-Asian infusion adds an intriguing, spicy edge to cocktails.

1 cup peeled and thinly sliced fresh ginger
One 750-ml bottle good-quality vodka

Place the ginger in a large glass container, add the vodka, and cap tightly. Let stand at room temperature for 48 hours, shaking gently once or twice a day. Taste for the preferred flavor intensity, allowing it to infuse for up to 2 more days if needed. (Do not allow it to infuse any longer than 2 weeks, or a bitter flavor will result.) Strain the infused vodka into the original bottle. Cap tightly, label, and refrigerate until ready to serve.

Cucumber Vodka

This infusion is fabulously refreshing in summer coolers and minimalist Martinis.

1 cup English (hothouse) cucumber, sliced
One 750-ml bottle good-quality vodka

Place the cucumber in a large glass container, add the vodka, and cap tightly. Let stand at room temperature for 3 weeks, shaking gently every couple of days. Taste for the preferred flavor intensity, allowing it to infuse for up to another week if needed. (Do not allow it to infuse any longer than 2 weeks, or a bitter flavor will result.) Strain the infused vodka into the original bottle. Cap tightly, label, and refrigerate until ready to serve.

Pepper Vodka

The hottest thing to ever hit a bottle of vodka, this infusion adds a perfect element of spicy boost guaranteed to produce the best damn Bloody Marys (page 35).

1 serrano chile, stemmed, seeded,
   and quartered lengthwise
1 jalapeño chile, stemmed, seeded,
   and quartered lengthwise
1 red habanero chile, stemmed, seeded,
   and quartered lengthwise
One 750-ml bottle good-quality vodka

Place the chiles in a large glass container, add the vodka, and cap tightly. Let stand at room temperature for 48 hours, shaking gently once or twice a day. Taste for the preferred flavor and heat intensity, allowing it to infuse for up to 2 more days if needed. (Do not allow it to infuse any longer than 2 weeks, or a bitter flavor will result.) Strain the infused vodka back into the original bottle. Cap tightly, label, and refrigerate until ready to serve.

Pineapple Vodka

This is the perfect infusion to give your tall summer coolers a sunny disposition. Look for prepared fresh sliced pineapple as an easy option to a whole pineapple.

1 whole fresh pineapple
One 750-ml bottle good-quality vodka

With a sharp knife, cut off the rind and core the pineapple. Cut the pineapple flesh into small cubes. Place the cubed pineapple in a large glass container, add the vodka, and cap tightly. Let stand at room temperature for 1 week, shaking gently every couple of days. Transfer to the refrigerator and infuse for another week, again shaking gently every couple of days. Taste for the preferred flavor intensity, allowing it to infuse for up to another week if needed. (Do not allow it to infuse any longer than 2 weeks, or a bitter flavor will result.) Strain the infused vodka into the original bottle. Cap tightly, label, and refrigerate until ready to serve.

Pink Grapefruit Vodka

This is pure pucker, made with sweet Texas Ruby Red grapefruit (or regular for more tartness) and refreshingly ready for a Grapefruit Martini or other summer cooler.

1 large pink grapefruit, unpeeled and sliced
One 750-ml bottle good-quality vodka

Place the grapefruit slices in a large glass container, add the vodka, and cap tightly. Let stand at room temperature for 1 week, shaking gently every couple of days. Taste for the preferred flavor intensity, allowing it to infuse for up to another week if needed. (Do not allow it to infuse any longer than 2 weeks, or a bitter flavor will result.) Strain the infused vodka into the original bottle. Cap tightly, label, and refrigerate until ready to serve.

Quadruple-Citrus Vodka

This super-citrusy infusion is highly versatile, giving a lively tang to cocktails. Use in any recipe calling for citron or other citrus vodkas.

1 grapefruit
1 orange
1 lime
1 lemon
One 750-ml bottle good-quality vodka

With a sharp paring knife, cut the peel off each citrus fruit in long, thin strips. Reserve the fruit for another use. Place the citrus peels in a large glass container, add the vodka, and cap tightly. Let stand at room temperature for 48 hours, shaking gently once or twice a day. Taste for the preferred flavor intensity, allowing it to infuse for up to 1 week if needed. (Do not allow it to infuse any longer than 2 weeks, or a bitter flavor will result.) Strain the infused vodka into the original bottle. Cap tightly, label, and refrigerate until ready to serve.

Raspberry Vodka

This berry infusion is great in fruity cocktails such as the Cosmopolitan (page 81). Try this recipe substituting 3 cups of your favorite berry for the raspberries, or for multidimensional flavor, add 1 cup firmly packed fresh mint or basil leaves to the berry infusion.

3 cups fresh raspberries
One 750-ml bottle good-quality vodka

Place the raspberries in a large glass container, add the vodka, and cap tightly. Let stand at room temperature for 1 week, shaking gently every couple of days. Taste for the preferred flavor intensity, allowing it to infuse for up to another week if needed. (Do not allow it to infuse any longer than 2 weeks or a bitter flavor will result.) Strain the infused vodka into the original bottle. Cap tightly, label, and refrigerate until ready to serve.

Strawberry Vodka

This infusion adds a sweet strawberry flavor to a variety of cocktails and is essential to the best Strawberry-Basil Martini (page 110).

3 cups fresh strawberries, hulled and sliced
One 750-ml bottle good-quality vodka

Place the strawberries in a large glass container, add the vodka, and cap tightly. Let stand at room temperature for 1 week, shaking gently every couple of days. Taste for the preferred flavor intensity, allowing it to infuse for up to another week if needed. (Do not allow it to infuse any longer than 2 weeks, or a bitter flavor will result.) Strain the infused vodka into the original bottle. Cap tightly, label, and refrigerate until ready to serve.

Watermelon Vodka

Use this infusion to add a fabulous melon twist to the classic Cosmopolitan (page 81) or give those tall, spritzy vodka coolers a great summery flavor. Try cantaloupe or honeydew melon in place of the watermelon, or for a tropical twist, add a mango or half a pineapple.

3 cups cubed fresh watermelon
One 750-ml bottle good-quality vodka

Place the watermelon in a large glass container, add the vodka, and cap tightly. Let stand at room temperature for 1 week, shaking gently every couple of days. Taste for the preferred flavor intensity, allowing it to infuse for up to another week if needed. (Don't allow it to infuse any longer than 2 weeks or a bitter flavor will result.) Strain the infused vodka into the original bottle. Cap tightly, label, and refrigerate until ready to serve.

Mango-Lemongrass Vodka

This infusion will give your Vodka Martini that Pacific Rim appeal.

2 ripe mangoes, peeled, pitted, and sliced
2 lemongrass stalks, cut into long pieces
One 750-ml bottle good-quality vodka

Place the mango and lemongrass pieces in a large glass container, add the vodka, and cap tightly. Let stand at room temperature for 1 week, shaking gently every couple of days. Taste for the preferred flavor intensity, allowing it to infuse for up to another week if needed. (Do not allow it to infuse any longer than 2 weeks, or a bitter flavor will result.) Strain the infused vodka into the original bottle. Cap tightly, label, and refrigerate until ready to serve.

Swank Rims

A glamorous edible dusting on the rim of a shimmering, frosted drink adds a certain *je ne sais quoi* excitement to the modern cocktail. Whether of cocoa powder, superfine sugar, or a tart savory mixture of salt and lime zest, rims bring texture, visual appeal, and instant elegance to a libation, along with enhancing the flavor.

The basic method of rimming a glass can be applied to a variety of ingredients. Ideally the glass should be chilled, but an unchilled glass will work in a pinch. You can prepare the rims ahead of time and have the rimmed glasses chilling in the refrigerator until needed.

Basic Rimming Method

1. Rub a lemon or lime wedge once around the rim of the glass to moisten it. Alternatively, dip the rim in a saucer of liqueur such as Grand Marnier, peppermint schnapps, Chambord, or Pernod to bring another exciting flavor element to the cocktail.

2. Pour 5 to 6 tablespoons of the rimming ingredient (such as salt or superfine sugar) onto a small plate or into a small, wide bowl and shake gently to distribute evenly.

3. Turn the glass upside down and set the moistened edge in the rimming ingredient. Gently rotate the glass back and forth to coat the rim completely, then shake off any excess.

4. Carefully pour in the cocktail, so as not to disturb the rim.

Salt Rim

For Bloody Marys, Salty Dogs, and Margaritas

Moisten the rim of the glass with a lime or lemon wedge, using sea salt for your rim, and proceed according to the basic method.

Sugar Rim

For a touch of sweetness that creates the perfect balance in tart cocktails such as a Lemon Drop.

Moisten the rim of the glass with a citrus wedge. Using superfine sugar for your rim, proceed according to the basic method. As an alternative to the citrus wedge, use Chambord for a pink rim, green crème de menthe for a green rim, and blue curaçao for a blue rim. You can use powdered sugar for a more delicate texture, or turbinado sugar for a bejeweled look that's a perfect for serving chocolate- or coffee-based cocktails.

Salt-and-Sugar Rim

For those who prefer a sweet-and-sour combination, this is a great rim for Margaritas or Daiquiris.

Moisten the rim of the glass with a lime wedge. Combine 3 tablespoons sea salt and 3 tablespoons granulated sugar for your rim and proceed according to the basic method.

Citrus Zest Rims

A rim of salt and lime zest enhances the usual salt-only Margarita rim, and mixing orange, lemon, and/or lime zests with sugar for rimming gives a flavor boost to your favorite citrus-based cocktail.

Moisten the rim of the glass with a complementary juice or liqueur. Combine 4 tablespoons granulated sugar or sea salt with 3 tablespoons finely grated orange, lemon, and/or lime zest for your rim and proceed according to the basic method. (Depending on the size of the glasses, the mixture will cover 3 or 4 rims.)

Grated Chocolate or Cocoa Powder Rims

Following the basic method, rim your Espresso Martini (page 82) or Chocolatini (page 79) with a few tablespoons of finely grated semisweet chocolate; this will add power to the chocolate punch or sweetness to slightly more bitter espresso- or coffee-liqueur-based drinks. This also comple-ments drinks with lemon or orange flavors. A cocoa powder rim is an elegant addition to cream or ice cream drinks; just a few tablespoons of unsweetened cocoa powder will coat several glasses. You also might want to try adding a ½ teaspoon of freshly grated nutmeg or ground cinnamon to the cocoa powder. For a fabulous chocolate-mint rim, simply dip the rim into peppermint schnapps or white crème de menthe, then into the cocoa powder.

Coconut Rim

A rim of finely grated fresh coconut, toasted, or dried un-sweetened coconut adds a textural touch to coconut-based and other tropical drinks. Moisten the rim of the glass with a complementary flavored liqueur such as Cointreau or Cham-bord, and proceed according to the basic method. (Half a cup of grated coconut will coat 3 or 4 rims.)

The Essential Syrups

Simple syrup is a great sweetening agent used in many mixed drinks and, unlike granulated sugar, requires no dissolving or excessive stirring to incorporate. It's also the base for sweet-and-sour syrup, a must-have staple behind the bar. Both syrups can be made ahead of time and refrigerated in a clean, covered jar for up to 2 weeks.

Simple Syrup

Also known as sugar syrup, this is an essential ingredient in many drinks. You can multiply the formula given here or cut it in half. Makes 2 cups.

1 cup water
2 cups sugar

In a small saucepan, bring the water to a boil. Remove from the heat, add the sugar, and stir until the sugar is completely dissolved. Let cool completely before using or refrigerating. Pour into a clean glass jar, cap tightly, and refrigerate for up to 2 weeks.

Sweet-and-Sour Syrup

This is one of those quick and convenient ready-made ingredients professional bartenders depend on. The combined sweet and citrus flavors make for a great shortcut mixture used in many drinks, including the Margarita. Forget about store-bought sweet-and-sour mixes; freshly made sweet-and-sour is the only way to go. For the best flavor, use spring or filtered water instead of tap water. Makes 2 cups.

½ cup cooled Simple Syrup (above)
¾ cup fresh lime juice
¾ cup fresh lemon juice
¼ cup water

Pour all of the ingredients into a clean glass jar with a tight-fitting lid. Close tightly and shake the contents together until well mixed. Refrigerate for up to 2 weeks.

The Classics
Quintessential Vodka Cocktails

No vodka book would be complete without including the classic cocktails that ushered vodka into the popular cocktail mainstream. Once the Moscow Mule and the Bloody Mary had been introduced into the American cocktail scene in the thirties and forties, vodka's popularity really took hold, and by the 1950s, the states witnessed an explosion of now-classic vodka cocktails, from the Screwdriver and the Greyhound to the Vodka Martini and the Black Russian. Here are our favorites that have withstood the test of time and are still sublime. All the recipes in this chapter and throughout the book serve one, but can easily be doubled or tripled to accommodate any size gathering.

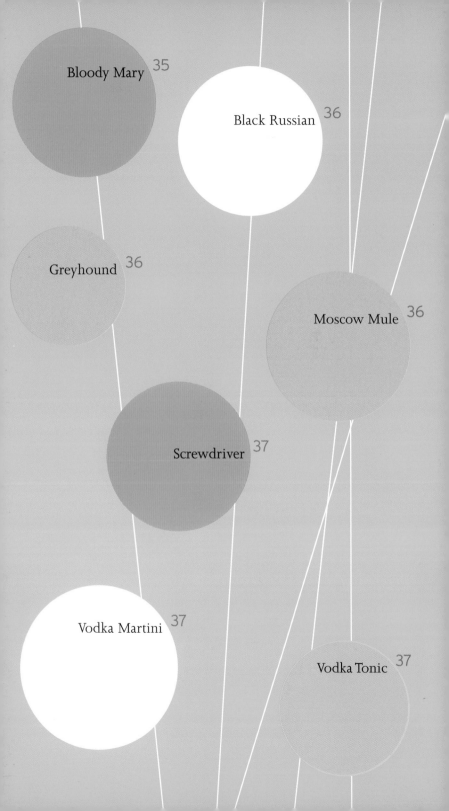

Bloody Mary 35

Black Russian 36

Greyhound 36

Moscow Mule 36

Screwdriver 37

Vodka Martini 37

Vodka Tonic 37

Bloody Mary

Lime wedge
Kosher salt
¼ teaspoon horseradish, preferably freshly grated
1 clove garlic, minced
1 green onion, white and tender green parts only,
    finely chopped
2 or 3 dashes Tabasco sauce
2 or 3 dashes Worcestershire sauce
½ ounce fresh lime juice
Freshly cracked black pepper to taste
2 ounces pepper vodka,
    homemade (page 22) or commercial
4 ounces tomato or V8 juice

Garnish:
1 lemon or lime wedge
1 green onion
1 celery stick

Rub the rim of a chilled highball glass with the lime wedge
and rim with the salt. (Alternatively, use a lime zest and salt
rim; see page 30.) Combine the horseradish, garlic, chopped
green onion, Tabasco, Worcestershire, lime juice, and cracked
pepper in the bottom of a cocktail shaker and muddle into
a lumpy paste. Add the vodka and tomato juice and shake
the ingredients vigorously with ice. Fill the rimmed highball
glass with ice, being careful not to disturb the rim. Strain
mixture into the ice-filled glass. Squeeze the lemon or lime
wedge over the drink and drop it in. Garnish with the whole
green onion and celery stick.

Black Russian

1½ ounces vodka
¾ ounce Kahlúa (or Tia Maria)

Garnish:
Lemon twist

Shake the liquid ingredients vigorously with ice. Strain into an ice-filled old-fashioned glass. Twist the lemon peel over the drink, and drop it in.

Greyhound

2 ounces good-quality vodka
5 to 6 ounces fresh grapefruit juice

Pour the ingredients into an ice-filled highball glass and stir.

Moscow Mule

2 ounces vodka
½ ounce fresh lime juice
4 ounces ginger beer (or ginger ale)

Garnish:
Lime wedge

Pour the vodka and lime juice into an ice-filled highball glass. Top with ginger beer and stir. Squeeze the lime wedge into the drink, and drop it in.

Screwdriver

2 ounces good-quality vodka
4 to 6 ounces fresh orange juice

Garnish:
1 orange slice

Pour the vodka and orange juice into an ice-filled highball glass and stir. Garnish with the orange slice.

Variation:
For a Slow Comfortable Screw, add ½ ounce sloe gin and ½ ounce Southern Comfort.

Vodka Martini

2 ounces vodka
½ ounce dry vermouth

Garnish:
Lemon twist (or green cocktail olive)

In a cocktail shaker, shake the liquid ingredients. Strain into a chilled cocktail glass. Run the lemon peel around the rim, twist it over the drink, and drop it in (or garnish with an olive).

Vodka Tonic

1 to 3 lime wedges
2 ounces vodka
3 to 5 ounces chilled tonic water

Rim a chilled highball glass with a lime wedge, and drop it in. Fill the glass with ice, pour in the vodka, and top with tonic water. Squeeze the remaining lime wedges into the drink.

From Russia with Love
Cold War Cocktails and Swinging Concoctions

Yes, it seems too cool to be true, but James Bond is almost single-handedly responsible for ushering the Vodka Martini into America's cocktail repertoire in the suburban dens of the Cold War era. Otherwise known as the Vodkatini, this clear, clean-tasting cocktail eclipsed the traditional Gin Martini in popularity by the late 1950s. A huge ad campaign undertaken by Smirnoff in conjunction with the macho Bond movies sent a strong message, promoting a stylish preference for Russian vodka into the mainstream of popular culture. Agent 007 also had a hand in changing the methodology of Martini drinking by requesting, in the film *Dr. No*, to have his "shaken not stirred," and thereby making it de rigueur to do so. Here is Bond's Martini, along with other gems from the fifties and sixties and a few fabulous elixirs inspired by the Age of Aquarius, to fuel your Summer of Love.

Vesper Martini

This infamous Martini was James Bond's cocktail of choice in Ian Fleming's classic *Casino Royale*. Named after Vesper Lynd, Bond's doomed double-agent girlfriend, it appropriately calls for Russian vodka, symbolic of Vesper Lynd's allegiance to the Soviets. Herbal-flavored Lillet Blanc, a French aperitif made from white wine, is a swank replacement for vermouth, and in our opinion, makes a more enjoyably complex Martini; serve, if you like, in Bond's preferred glass, a champagne coupe (similar in shape to a Martini glass, but with a shallower and more rounded bowl). Of course, this drink is shaken, not stirred.

Although Smirnoff was the promotional vodka linked with the James Bond movies, we prefer to use either Stolichnaya Gold or a favorite super-premium such as Belvedere or Ketel One.

1½ ounces gin
½ ounce premium Russian vodka
⅓ ounce Lillet Blanc

Garnish:
1 large orange- or lemon-peel twist

In a cocktail shaker, shake the liquid ingredients vigorously with ice. Strain into a chilled champagne coupe or cocktail glass. Twist the citrus peel over the drink and drop it in.

Dr. No's Dreamsicle

We all know that Dr. No had his regressive adolescent tendencies, and this decadent cocktail is right there, reminding us of our cravings brought on by the sound of neighborhood ice-cream trucks.

1 ounce amaretto
½ ounce orange curaçao
½ ounce vanilla vodka,
    homemade (page 20) or commercial
2 ounces fresh orange juice
2 ounces heavy cream

Garnish:
1 small fresh mint sprig

In a cocktail shaker, shake the liquid ingredients vigorously with ice. Strain into an ice-filled old-fashioned glass. Garnish with the mint sprig.

Bombay Barbarella

The name says it all—fragrant yet brazen, just like our sixties galactic über-chick Barbarella. The flavors in this fabulous cocktail are perfectly balanced between the strong and the delicate; Bombay-inspired, the vanilla, citrus, and exotic spicy tones will send you into cosmic karma ecstasy.

1½ ounces vanilla vodka,
    homemade (page 20) or commercial
Tiny splash of amaretto
1½ ounces fresh orange juice
¼ ounce fresh lime juice
¼ ounce Simple Syrup (page 31)
2 to 3 thin slices fresh ginger
4 whole cloves

Garnish:
1 small, thin orange slice
1 piece candied ginger

In a cocktail shaker, shake all the ingredients except the garnishes vigorously with ice. Strain into a chilled cocktail glass. Float the orange slice on top and place candied ginger on the rim.

Variation:
For a frosty, creamy version, substitute ¼ cup orange sorbet for the orange juice and combine in a blender.

Goldfinger

Inspired by the classic sixties concoction, we added a cinnamony twist with the visually appropriate Goldschläger liqueur, a cinnamon schnapps with trademark gold flecks. Stoli Gold is a good choice for the vodka.

1½ ounces good-quality Russian vodka
¾ ounce Galliano
1 ounce pineapple juice
½ ounce Goldschläger

In a cocktail shaker, shake the vodka, Galliano, and pineapple juice vigorously with ice. Strain into a chilled cocktail glass. Float the Goldschläger on top.

White Cloud

This classic covers both tropical longings and chocolate urges beautifully.

1½ ounces good-quality vodka
¾ ounce crème de cacao
2 ounces pineapple juice
¾ ounce heavy cream

In a cocktail shaker, shake the ingredients vigorously with ice. Strain into an ice-filled highball glass.

Octuplushy

Raspberry red and divine, sip this liquid
velvet dynamite slowly.

1 ounce raspberry vodka,
   homemade (page 24) or commercial
¾ ounce crème de cassis
1½ ounces fresh lime juice
½ ounce fresh lemon juice
½ ounce Simple Syrup (page 31)

Garnish:
2 fresh raspberries

In a cocktail shaker, shake the liquid ingredients vigorously
with ice. Strain into a chilled cocktail glass. Garnish with the
raspberries.

Ocean's Eleven

A modernistic hybrid of high-octane high-balls, this is one cool breeze of a drink, conjuring up the swinging, ultra-cool Rat Pack, who set the party tone for the sixties while leisurely sipping their cocktails by a Vegas pool.

2 ounces Pink Grapefruit Vodka (page 23)
1 ounce Galliano
2 ounces fresh grapefruit juice
1 ounce fresh orange juice

Garnish:
1 small, thin orange slice

In a cocktail shaker, shake the liquid ingredients vigorously with ice. Strain into an ice-filled highball glass. Garnish by placing the orange slice on the rim.

Variation:
For an Ocean's Eleven Martini, shake and serve up in a cocktail glass; moisten the rim with Galliano and rim with sugar (see page 29).

For the Hollywood "star" treatment, rub the rim of a highball glass with a slice of orange, and then dip in sugar (see page 29). Fill the glass with ice, stir in the liquid ingredients, and garnish with a slice of star fruit, sprinkled with coarse sugar.

In-a-Vodka-Da-Vida
Orgasmic Shooters and Fuzzy Headbangers

The 1970s were all about regression, the "me" generation, and the arrival of sweet, fruity, liqueur-heavy drinks that masked any trace of alcohol—for which vodka, with its tasteless cameleonlike nature, was the ideal base. The era's taste for adolescent "sensation" drinks—sexual innuendos in a glass producing candied intoxication in all the right creamy, disco-licious ways—has never really gone away. From Wallbangers to Cadillacs and Orgasms to Quaaludes, we have it all here, baby, including a few fabulous seventies-inspired newbies of our own.

Orgasmic Shooters 50	Screaming Orgasm 51	
Woo Woo 51	Sex on the Beach 52	Liquid Cocaine 54
Buttery Nipple 54	Brain Hemorrhage 55	Russian Quaalude 55
Fuzzy Headbangers 56	Harvey Wallbanger 57	Foxy Brown 59
Flying Grasshopper 60	International Incident 61	Climax 61
Pink Cadillac 62	Purple Passion 65	Kitty Carlyle 66
Tropical Cadillac 67	Pink Squirrel 67	Windex 68

Orgasmic Shooters

Evidently the criteria for the titillating and popular Seventies shooter was to make the most sweet-liqueur-intensive shot possible with an ounce or so of vodka hidden within and give it a sexually provocative or disgusting name, to pack a mini-wallop. These classics accomplish the task splendidly.

Screaming Orgasm

What makes you orgasmic is subjective, of course, but many insist on chocolate, so we thought a float of Godiva chocolate liqueur was the perfect addition to this classic shot.

½ ounce good-quality vodka
½ ounce amaretto
½ ounce Baileys Irish Cream
½ ounce Kahlúa or Tia Maria
¼ ounce Godiva chocolate liqueur or crème de cacao

In a cocktail shaker, shake all the ingredients except the chocolate liqueur vigorously with ice. Strain into a chilled shot glass. Float the chocolate liqueur on top. Drink down in one gulp.

Woo Woo

A classic shooter inspired by the Sea Breeze and Madras genre.

½ ounce well-chilled good-quality vodka
½ ounce peach schnapps
½ ounce cranberry juice

Pour the ingredients into a chilled shot glass. Drink down in one gulp.

Variation:
Increase the vodka to 1¼ ounces, the schnapps to ¾ ounce, and the cranberry juice to 3 ounce. Shake all the ingredients vigorously with ice. Shake and serve up in a chilled cocktail glass or in an ice-filled highball glass.

Sex on the Beach

There are as many different transmutations
of this classic as there are ways to, well,
enjoy sex on the beach. Here are two fruity
and potent versions that have had their illus-
trious day in the sun.

Sex on the Beach #1

$1/2$ ounce good-quality vodka
$1/2$ ounce peach schnapps
$1/2$ ounce fresh orange juice
$1/2$ ounce cranberry juice

Garnish:
2 cherries (optional)

In a cocktail shaker, shake the ingredients vigorously with
ice. Strain into a chilled shot glass and drop in a cherry or
two, if you like. Drink down in one gulp.

Sex on the Beach #2

$1/2$ ounce good-quality vodka
$1/2$ ounce Chambord
$1/2$ ounce Midori or other melon liqueur
$1/2$ ounce pineapple juice

In a cocktail shaker, shake the ingredients vigorously with
ice. Strain into a chilled shot glass. Drink down in one gulp.

Liquid Cocaine

Seeing as there are many versions of this drink, we took the opportunity to experiment ourselves, substituting vodka for the usual dark rum. The results are fabulous. Rumple Minze is a 100-proof, very strong-flavored peppermint schnapps from Germany.

½ ounce good-quality vodka
½ ounce root beer schnapps
½ ounce Jägermeister
½ ounce Rumple Minze

In a cocktail shaker, shake the ingredients vigorously with ice. Strain into a chilled shot glass and drink down in one gulp, or serve in an ice-filled old-fashioned glass.

Variation:
For a glittering version, substitute ½ ounce Goldschläger for the root beer schnapps.

Buttery Nipple

You just have to wonder what the story was behind the conception of this little beauty.

½ ounce well-chilled, good-quality vodka
½ ounce Baileys Irish Cream
½ ounce butterscotch schnapps

Pour the ingredients into a chilled shot glass. Drink down in one gulp.

Brain Hemorrhage

The trick to achieving the textural illusion of a "coagulation" is to pour the Irish crème in slowly, and then dribble a few drops of grenadine on top.

1 ounce well-chilled, good-quality vodka
½ ounce peach schnapps
½ ounce Baileys Irish Cream
2 to 3 drops grenadine

Pour the vodka and peach schnapps into a chilled shot glass. Slowly add the Baileys. Dribble the grenadine on top. Drink down in one gulp.

Russian Quaalude

One of the first creamy shots to mix international metaphors.

¾ ounce good-quality vodka
¾ ounce Frangelico
¾ ounce Baileys Irish Cream

In a cocktail shaker, shake the ingredients vigorously with ice. Strain into a chilled shot glass and drink down in one gulp.

Variations:
Serve layered as a pousse-café drink, carefully pouring in each ingredient in the order given, or shake and serve stylishly up in a chilled cocktail glass.

Fuzzy Headbangers

This select collection of fantastic cocktails, whether straight from a seventies
bar menu or inspired by them, are quint-
essentially sweet, creamy, and potent—
and still got what it takes, baby!

Harvey Wallbanger

This 1970s classic concoction evolved from a questionable story spun by the Galliano producers. It involved a California surfer named, you got it, Harvey, who, as the story goes, in the late sixties was hell-bent on nursing a few screwdrivers after he lost a surfing contest, and thought a splash of Galliano would be a consoling addition. Well, after quite a few of these he was staggering into walls and furniture, earning himself the nickname "wallbanger," which became synonymous with the new concoction. Whether or not this was indeed the moment of conception, we like the story anyway, and it is the anise-lover's answer to the basic Screwdriver.

1½ ounces good-quality vodka
4 to 5 ounces fresh orange juice
½ ounce Galliano

In a cocktail shaker, shake the vodka and orange juice vigorously with ice. Strain into an ice-filled highball glass. Float the Galliano on top.

Variation:
For a classic Brass Monkey, add ½ ounce light rum.

Foxy Brown

This energizing urban, street-savvy cocktail is just as sexy and full of attitude as Foxy herself. Straight from hip-central, Saucebox, a swank restaurant and bar in Portland, Oregon, this decadent concoction is tailor-made to fit the delicious criteria of a quint-essentially seventies cocktail.

1½ ounces vanilla vodka,
    homemade (page 20) or commercial
½ ounce Godiva chocolate liqueur
1 ounce strong iced coffee

Garnish:
Dollop of whipped cream
Pinch each of ground cinnamon and freshly ground nutmeg

In a cocktail shaker, shake the vodka, chocolate liqueur, and coffee vigorously with ice. Strain into a chilled cocktail glass. Top with a dollop of whipped cream and sprinkle with the cinnamon and nutmeg.

Flying Grasshopper

Also simply called the Grasshopper, we've upgraded this 1970s classic with a few fresh mint leaves and Godiva white chocolate liqueur—the green crème de menthe is essential to the "grasshopper" symbolism.

1½ ounces good-quality vodka
1½ ounces Godiva white chocolate liqueur
1 ounce green crème de menthe
1 ounce heavy cream
2 to 3 fresh small mint sprigs

Garnish:
1 small fresh mint sprig

In a cocktail shaker, shake all the ingredients except the garnish vigorously with ice. Strain into an ice-filled old-fashioned glass or chilled cocktail glass. Garnish with the mint sprig.

Variations:
For a super-creamy, frothy version, in a blender, combine the ingredients with 1½ ounces heavy cream and ½ cup of ice, and blend until smooth.

For a Japanese Grasshopper, add ½ ounce Midori.

International Incident

True to the times, this seventies classic dip-lomatically covers just about every favorite sweet liqueur known to pair nicely with java and is guaranteed to get you buzzing.

1½ ounces good-quality vodka
1 ounce Baileys Irish Cream
¼ ounce amaretto
¼ ounce Frangelico
2 ounces cold coffee

Garnish:
1 small, thin orange slice

In a cocktail shaker, shake all the liquid ingredients vigor-ously with ice. Strain into an ice-filled highball glass. Garnish with the orange slice placed on the rim.

Climax

This is indeed an orgasmic combination of heady liqueurs, to be sipped and savored as long as you can keep it up—your glass, of course.

1 ounce good-quality vodka
½ ounce amaretto
½ ounce Cointreau
½ ounce crème de banane
½ ounce crème de cacao
1 ounce heavy cream

In a cocktail shaker, shake the ingredients vigorously with ice. Strain into an ice-filled old-fashioned glass or chilled cocktail glass.

Pink Cadillac

In swinging seventies speak, any drink with "Cadillac" at the end of its name usually meant it was laced with Galliano, that sexy Euro-stylish anise-flavored liqueur. This is a refined version of the original—slightly creamy and super zingy!

1 1/2 ounces good-quality vodka
3/4 ounce Chambord
1/4 ounce Galliano
1 ounce Sweet-and-Sour Syrup (page 31)
1 ounce half-and-half

Garnish:
1 small, thin orange slice
1 fresh raspberry

In a cocktail shaker, shake the ingredients vigorously with ice. Strain into a chilled cocktail glass. Garnish with a skewered raspberry and orange slice.

Variations:
For a souped-up Pink Cadillac, dip the rim in Chambord and rim with sugar (see page 29).

For a Russian Cadillac, substitute white crème de cacao for the Chambord.

Purple Passion

We've taken the liberty of modernizing this classic grape-imbued drink. Made with Ciroc grape vodka and a whisper of sweet Parfait Amour, it will spark a passion for another round.

1½ ounces Ciroc grape vodka
1 ounce grape juice
½ ounce Parfait Amour (violet liqueur)
½ ounce fresh grapefruit juice
1 teaspoon Simple Syrup (page 31)

In a cocktail shaker, shake the ingredients vigorously with ice. Strain into a chilled cocktail glass.

Variation:
For added romance, serve this drink in a martini glass rimmed with sugar (see page 29) and a garnish of sugared grapes.

Kitty Carlyle

Just like the lady it's named after, this drink is swank and saucy; we think it belongs in the pantheon of great cocktails. Created by master mixologist Felicia Sledge, it's a fabulously spicy blend of ginger and apple cider that is zingy and refreshing—and don't even *think* of using plain apple juice, it's just not the same.

1½ ounces Ginger Vodka (page 21)
1 ounce fresh lemon juice
¼ ounce Simple Syrup (page 31)
1½ ounces apple cider

Garnish:
1 thin lemon slice

In a cocktail shaker, shake the vodka, lemon juice, and Simple Syrup vigorously with ice. Strain into an ice-filled highball glass and float the apple cider on top. Garnish with the lemon slice placed on the rim.

Variations:
For a spritzy version, use sparkling apple cider in place of the regular.

For a Kitty Carlyle Martini, serve it up in a cocktail glass rimmed with sugar and lemon zest (see page 30).

Tropical Cadillac

A lush, tropical version of the Pink Cadillac to send your senses to the beach.

1½ ounces good-quality vodka
½ ounce Galliano
½ ounce crème de cassis
1 ounce pineapple juice
½ ounce fresh lime juice

In a cocktail shaker, shake the ingredients vigorously with ice. Strain into a chilled cocktail glass.

Pink Squirrel

This classic is traditionally made with crème de noyaux, a crème liqueur with an almond flavor, and typically shaken, but it's also divine when blended with a handful of ice and, if you like, a small scoop of vanilla ice cream.

1½ ounces good-quality vodka
1 ounce white crème de cacao
1 ounce creme de noyaux
1 ounce heavy cream

In a cocktail shaker, shake all the ingredients vigorously with ice. Strain into a chilled cocktail glass.

Windex

The perfect seventies antidote for housewives needing a reviving "Mother's little helper" after a long day slaving over avocado-hued appliances.

1½ ounces good-quality vodka
½ ounce Cointreau
½ ounce blue curaçao
2 ounces Sweet-and-Sour Syrup (page 31)
3 to 4 ounces chilled lemon-lime soda

Garnish:
1 lemon wedge

Pour all of the liquid ingredients but the soda into an ice-filled highball glass. Stir well. Top with the soda. Squeeze the lemon wedge into the drink and drop it in.

Variation:
The Windex can also be served "up" with a sugared rim (see page 29) and a slice of lemon for garnish.

Modern Classics
The New Urban Cocktail Legends

The moment of conception of the Cosmopolitan in the late 1980s seemed to spark a creative revolution of mixology, producing a whole new breed of modern cocktail legends served elegantly in a frosty martini glass or refreshingly over ice. Crafted with well-balanced flavors and an alchemic clarity, these are the new American classics.

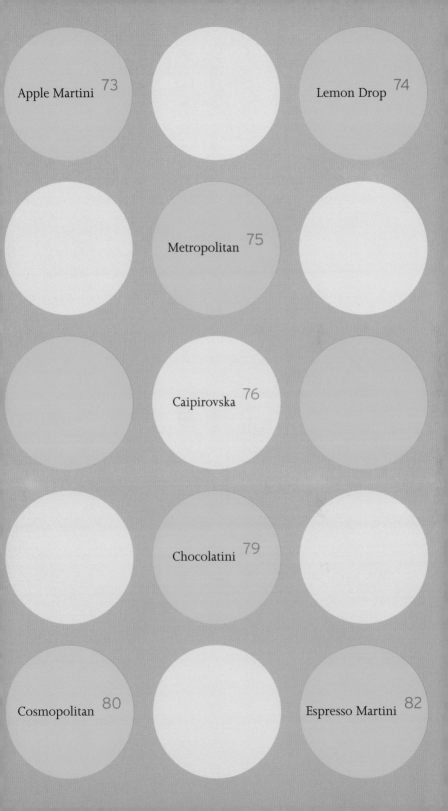

Apple Martini 73

Lemon Drop 74

Metropolitan 75

Caipirovska 76

Chocolatini 79

Cosmopolitan 80

Espresso Martini 82

Apple Martini

Relatively new on the scene, this cocktail was first served at Lola's in L.A. and called the Adam's Apple Martini after the bartender. Simultaneously sweet and puckery-tart, with extreme apple flavor, it has become quite the rage.

¼ cup peeled, diced apple or 1 ounce apple juice
¼ ounce fresh lemon juice
1½ ounces good-quality vodka or apple vodka
½ ounce green apple schnapps

Garnish:
1 or 2 thin apple slices

Muddle the apple and lemon juice together in the bottom of a cocktail shaker. Add the vodka and schnapps, and shake vigorously with ice. Strain into a chilled cocktail glass. Garnish with the apple slices placed on the rim.

Variations:
For a spicier version, substitute the homemade Green Apple-Clove Vodka (page 18) for the regular vodka, or try the Spiced Apple Martini.

Spiced Apple Martini

1½ ounces Zubrowka Bison grass vodka
½ ounce green apple liqueur
¼ ounce butterscotch schnapps
¼ ounce fresh lemon juice

In a cocktail shaker, shake the ingredients vigorously with ice. Strain into a chilled cocktail glass.

Lemon Drop

Dangerously delicious, this candy-esque cocktail goes down sooo easy—a few can pack a wallop, so keep count. We think this is the most fabulous lemon drop recipe, with the perfect balance of sweet and tart. To up the frosty factor, put the vodka in the freezer for a couple hours, until icy cold.

1 lemon wedge
Superfine sugar
1½ ounces citron vodka
1 ounce Grand Marnier or Cointreau
1½ ounces fresh lemon juice
½ ounce fresh orange juice

Garnish:
1 lemon peel spiral

Rub the rim of a large chilled cocktail glass with the lemon wedge and rim with sugar (see page 29). In a cocktail shaker, shake the liquid ingredients vigorously with ice. Strain carefully into the prepared glass. Garnish with the lemon spiral.

Variation:
For a Bullfrog, strain into an ice-filled highball glass. Top with club soda. Squeeze a wedge of lemon into the drink and drop it in.

Metropolitan

The conception of this very berry-flavored variation on the Cosmopolitan is attributed to the mixologist Chuck Coggins, who was shaking these little gems back in the 1990s behind the bar at Marion's in New York. The original recipe was made without the Cointreau, but we prefer this enhanced version.

2 ounces black currant vodka
¾ ounce Cointreau
¾ ounce cranberry juice
¾ ounce fresh lime juice

Garnish:
1 small lime wedge

In a cocktail shaker, shake the liquid ingredients vigorously with ice. Strain into a chilled cocktail glass. Squeeze the lime wedge over the top of the drink and drop in.

Caipirovska

Russia's answer to the Brazilian classic. This refreshing Caipirinha-inspired drink, made with vodka instead of the traditional cachaça, is a sweeter option to the basic Vodka Tonic. Many enjoy this with a splash of club soda as well.

1 small lime, cut into 8 wedges
1 tablespoon sugar
2 ounces premium vodka

Muddle the lime with the sugar in the bottom of an old-fashioned glass. Fill the glass with crushed ice, add the vodka, and stir well.

Variation:
For an Orange Caipirovska, substitute orange or mandarin vodka for the regular vodka and a few small orange and lemon wedges for the lime.

Chocolatini

Finally, a martini for the chocoholic. This decadent cocktail is the ultimate fix and is made more sublime when Godiva chocolate liqueur is used instead of the usual dark crème de cacao. To really send you into chocolate bliss, use a cocoa powder rim (see page 30).

1½ ounces good-quality vodka
    or vanilla vodka, homemade (page 20) or commercial
¼ ounce Godiva chocolate liqueur
    or dark crème de cacao
¼ ounce white crème de cacao

Garnish:
Bittersweet chocolate shavings

In a cocktail shaker, shake the liquid ingredients vigorously with ice. Strain into a chilled cocktail glass. Sprinkle the chocolate shavings over the top.

Variations:
For a Clear Chocolate Martini, substitute white crème de cacao for the Godiva.

For a White Chocolate Martini, rim the glass with powdered sugar (see page 29), substitute Godiva white chocolate liqueur for the regular chocolate Godiva,

For a Mandarin Chocolate Martini, rub the rim with an orange wedge and rim with unsweetened cocoa powder (see page 30). Increase the Godiva liqueur to 1 ounce and substitute ¼ ounce Mandarine Napoleon liqueur for the crème de cacao.

Cosmopolitan

The extremely popular "Cosmo" was the hot new cocktail in the late eighties, then the signature drink of the *Sex and the City* set, and now a firmly established classic. The creator is unknown and the origins somewhat hazy; around the mid-1980s, Julie's Supper Club in San Francisco was serving a drink called the Cosmopolitan, and then in the late 1980s, a high-profile version of the new pink drink was concocted by Toby Cecchini at the Odeon Bar in New York. Toby changed the vodka to citron vodka, which became de rigueur as the Cosmo became *the* drink to order: a refreshingly tart concoction of citron vodka, lime juice, Cointreau to take the edge off the lime, and cranberry juice used merely to add a slight blush of color. These days you will find that most recipes have evolved into sweeter, deep pink variations heavy on the cranberry juice; we prefer the lighter-handed original, but here are both versions from which to choose your particular cranberry quotient.

Original Cosmopolitan

1 ½ ounces citron vodka,
 or homemade Quadruple-Citrus Vodka (page 24)
1 ½ ounces Cointreau
1 ounce fresh lime juice
1 or 2 dashes cranberry juice

Garnish:
1 lemon peel twist

In a cocktail shaker, shake the liquid ingredients vigorously with ice. Strain into a chilled cocktail glass. Twist the lemon peel over the drink and drop it in.

Cranberri-licious Cosmopolitan

This is the cranberry lover's version. Try substituting homemade citrus-infused vodka instead of the classic citron vodka, to impart an extra citrusy dimension.

1 ½ ounces citron vodka,
 or homemade Quadruple-Citrus Vodka (page 24)
1 ounce Cointreau
1 ounce cranberry juice
½ ounce fresh lime juice

Garnish:
1 lime peel twist or 2 cranberries

In a cocktail shaker, shake the liquid ingredients vigorously with ice. Strain into a chilled cocktail glass. Twist the lemon peel over the drink and drop it in, or drop in the cranberries.

Variations:
For a Mandarin Cosmo, substitute mandarin vodka for the citron, and Mandarine Napoléon liqueur for the Cointreau, and add a splash of mandarin orange juice.

For those who prefer non-pink drinks, there is the White Cosmo, made with white cranberry juice instead of the regular.

Espresso Martini

A coffee lover's dream; aromatic, energetic, and intense enough to stimulate a night of riotous behavior.

1½ ounces good-quality vodka
   or vanilla vodka, homemade (page 20) or commercial
½ ounce espresso or strong coffee
½ ounce Kahlúa
½ ounce crème de cacao

Garnish:
3 espresso beans

In a cocktail shaker, shake the liquid ingredients vigorously with ice. Strain into a chilled cocktail glass. Drop in the espresso beans.

Variation:
For a Javanese Martini, rim the glass with turbinado sugar (see page 29), substitute 1 ounce Tia Maria for the Kahlúa, omit the crème de cacao, and garnish with a lemon twist.

Swank Summer Coolers
Highballs for the Patio

When it's 100 degrees in the shade, and you need to quench your thirst with something long, tall, and frosty, you can count on these coolers to have it all: evocative flavors, style, and total refreshment.

Citrus Vanilla Sky 87

Cynar Cooler 88

Paradise Fizz 89

Melon Ball 90

Moscow Mojito 93

Mango Madras 94

The Italian Job 95

Pimm's Splash 96

Watermelon Fizz 99

Citrus Vanilla Sky

Superfabulistic and tart, this great summer quencher is made with our citrusy, spicy kumquat-and-vanilla-infused vodka. Serve over ice in a tall glass, or up in a chilled cocktail glass rimmed with sugar (see page 29) for a bit of glam; to add a touch of effervescent elegance, top with a splash of chilled Champagne. This cocktail is also great if made with just Vanilla Vodka (page 20), but either vodka will complement Tuaca's vanilla-orange flavor.

1½ ounces Kumquat-Vanilla Vodka (page 21)
½ ounce Tuaca
1 ounce fresh lime juice
½ ounce fresh grapefruit juice
¼ ounce Simple Syrup (page 31)

Garnish:
2 kumquat slices (optional)
1 vanilla bean (optional)

In a cocktail shaker, shake all the liquid ingredients vigorously with ice. Strain into an ice-filled highball glass. If you like, float the kumquat slices on top of the drink or garnish with a vanilla bean.

Cynar Cooler

For a touch of the exotic, try this surprisingly delicious combination of citrus juice and Cynar, a subtle and aromatic artichoke liqueur from Italy. This is another fantastic quenching concoction from master mixologist Felicia Sledge.

1½ ounces good-quality vodka
½ ounce Cynar
½ ounce fresh lemon juice
½ ounce fresh orange juice
2 to 3 ounces chilled club soda

Garnish:
1 small, thin orange slice

In a cocktail shaker, shake the vodka, Cynar, and lemon and orange juices vigorously with ice. Strain into an ice-filled highball glass. Top with the club soda and garnish with the orange slice placed on the rim.

Paradise Fizz

Appealing to your more decadent urges, tangy orange flavors come together with chocolate in this bubbly glass of paradise on ice——guaranteed to loosen any inhibitions at your next patio soirée. Created by master mixologist Mittie Hellmich.

1½ ounces good-quality vodka
½ ounce Tuaca
½ ounce white crème de cacao
2 to 3 ounces chilled sparkling tangerine
   or orange beverage

Garnish:
1 small, thin orange slice
1 small fresh mint sprig

In a cocktail shaker, shake the vodka, Tuaca, and crème de cacao vigorously with ice. Strain into an ice-filled highball glass. Top with the sparkling beverage. Garnish with the orange slice and mint placed on the rim.

Melon Ball

Midori is a bright chartreuse-hued, sweet muskmelon-flavored liqueur from Japan, and it adds a whisper of melon flavor to the classic summer Madras.

1 ounce good-quality vodka
1 ounce Midori or other melon liqueur
2 ounces fresh orange juice
1 ounce cranberry juice

Garnish:
1 small, thin orange slice
1 small, thin honeydew melon wedge

In a cocktail shaker, shake the liquid ingredients vigorously with ice. Strain into an ice-filled wineglass. Garnish with the orange slice and honeydew melon wedge.

Variation:
For a Melon Breeze: Substitute cranberry vodka for the regular vodka and fresh grapefruit juice for the orange juice.

Moscow Mojito

The Mojito was one of Hemingway's favorite Cuban cocktails, so he probably rolled in his grave when we replaced the rum with vodka—not to mention our addition of kumquats in our variation. This refreshing summer drink is best made with good-quality vodka and fresh mint; our version adds a splash of club soda.

1 ounce fresh lime juice
1 tablespoon superfine sugar
6 to 8 fresh mint leaves
2 ounces good-quality vodka
3 to 4 ounces chilled club soda

Garnish:
1 small fresh mint sprig

In the bottom of a highball glass, muddle together the lime juice, sugar, and mint leaves until the sugar is dissolved. Add the vodka. Fill the glass with ice and top with the club soda. Garnish with the mint sprig.

Variations:
For a Kumquat Mojito, substitute Kumquat-Vanilla Vodka (page 21) for the regular and muddle with 2 or 3 sliced kumquats.

For a Berrylicious Moscow Mojito, substitute Raspberry Vodka (page 24) for the regular.

For a Moscow Mojito Royale, top with chilled Champagne in place of the club soda.

Mango Madras

This tropical spritzer seems too luscious and refreshing to be legal. Made with ripe mango and tart grapefruit vodka, wow—summer coolers just don't get any better than this!

¼ cup peeled, pitted, and diced ripe mango
   or 2 ounces mango nectar
1½ ounces Pink Grapefruit Vodka (page 23)
Splash of cranberry juice
2 to 3 ounces chilled club soda

Garnish:
1 thin mango slice

Muddle the mango in the bottom of a cocktail shaker. Add the vodka and cranberry juice, and shake vigorously with ice. Strain into an ice-filled wineglass. Top with the club soda and garnish with the mango slice placed on the rim.

Variation:
For over-the-top Mango-a-go-go: Substitute Mango-Lemongrass Vodka (page 27) for the grapefruit vodka.

The Italian Job

Campari not only adds a great touch of bitterness to any cocktail, but also a glowing, ruby-red hue. It balances out the sweet and the tart, pairing perfectly with the grapefruit and orange flavors of this eye-catching jewel of a cocktail.

2 ounces Pink Grapefruit Vodka (page 23)
1 ounce Cointreau
½ ounce Campari
1 ounce fresh grapefruit juice
½ ounce fresh orange juice

Garnish:
1 small, thin orange slice

In a cocktail shaker, shake all the liquid ingredients vigorously with ice. Strain into an ice-filled highball glass. Garnish with the orange slice placed on the rim.

Variations:
Rim a cocktail glass with sugar (see page 29). Strain into the prepared glass and garnish with an orange peel twist.

For a spritzy version, top with sparkling grapefruit beverage.

Pimm's Splash

We started with the perennial English favorite and gave it an absolutely fabulous contemporary twist, using aromatic cucumber vodka and Lemoncello liqueur along with the traditional splash of herbally infused Pimm's No. 1.

1½ ounces Cucumber Vodka (page 22)
½ ounce Pimm's No. 1
¼ ounce Lemoncello
3 to 4 ounces chilled Champagne

Garnish:
1 thin cucumber slice

In a cocktail shaker, shake all the liquid ingredients except the Champagne vigorously with ice. Strain into an ice-filled highball glass. Top with the Champagne and stir briefly. Garnish with the cucumber slice.

Watermelon Fizz

Watermelon vodka is the only way to go for this refreshing *agua fresca*–esque drink, infusing it with the sweet taste of summer.

2 ounces Watermelon Vodka (page 25)
1 ounce Sweet-and-Sour Syrup (page 31)
Splash of cranberry juice
2 to 3 ounces chilled Champagne

Garnish:
1 small fresh mint sprig
1 thin lemon slice

In a cocktail shaker, shake the vodka, Sweet-and-Sour Syrup, and cranberry juice vigorously with ice. Strain into an ice-filled wineglass. Top with the Champagne and garnish with the lemon slice and a mint sprig placed on the rim.

Martini Madness
Innovation in Martini Mixology

The term "martini" no longer applies just to gin or vodka shaken or stirred with a whisper of dry vermouth; it is now used for just about anything served up in a cocktail glass. With that in mind, here are some of the best creative and innovative "Martinis" around, made with lush ingredients that are sublimely balanced for superswanky contemporary cocktails.

102
Blood
Orange
Martini

104
Bellini
Martini

105
Chocolate-
Mint
Martini

107
Blue
Crush

108
Love
Potion #9

109
Peartini

110
Strawberry-
Basil
Martini

112
Pink
Pussycat

113
Raspberry
Martini

115
Suntory
Cocktail

116
The Big O

Blood Orange Martini

This is the exotic cousin of the Lemon Drop, made sweet-tart and seductive with ruby red blood orange juice and a whisper of fragrant orange flower water.

1 orange wedge
Superfine sugar
1½ ounces orange vodka
1½ ounces fresh blood orange juice
¼ ounce Mandarine Napoléon or other orange liqueur
¼ ounce Lillet Blanc (see Vesper Martini, page 40)
Drop of orange flower water

Garnish:
1 blood orange slice

Rub the rim of a large chilled cocktail glass with the orange wedge and rim with sugar (see page 29). In a cocktail shaker, shake the liquid ingredients vigorously with ice. Strain carefully into the prepared glass. Garnish with the orange slice.

Bellini Martini

The inspiration for this delicious martini is the famous Italian Bellini cocktail, created in the 1940s in Venice, at Harry's Bar, in honor of the Venetian Renaissance painter Giovanni Bellini. Ideally made with fresh white peaches and prosecco (an Italian dry sparkling wine), regular peaches and Champagne are perfectly acceptable. You can also use peach nectar in place of the fresh peaches.

¼ cup peeled and diced ripe white peaches
   or 3 ounces peach nectar
1 ounce premium vodka
1 to 2 ounces chilled prosecco
   or other dry sparkling wine

Garnish:
1 peach slice

Muddle the peaches in the bottom of a cocktail shaker. Add the vodka and shake vigorously with ice. Strain into a chilled cocktail glass. Slowly float the prosecco on top. Garnish with the fresh peach slice placed on the rim.

Chocolate-Mint Martini

What could be better than a chocolate martini? Mint, of course, just a hint, just a whisper to remind you that it *can* "get better than this."

1½ ounces vanilla vodka,
    homemade (see page 20) or commercial
1 ounce dark crème de cacao
2 or 3 fresh mint leaves

Garnish:
1 small fresh mint sprig

In a cocktail shaker, shake the vodka, crème de cacao, and mint leaves vigorously with ice. Strain into a chilled cocktail glass. Garnish with the mint sprig.

Variations:
For a Chocolate-Coconut Martini, omit the mint and add ½ ounce coconut milk.

For a Chocolate-Raspberry Mint Martini, substitute Raspberry Vodka (page 24) for the vanilla, and add ¼ ounce Chambord.

For a Malted Milk Martini, omit the mint and add ¼ ounce amaretto, 1 teaspoon malted milk powder, and ½ ounce heavy cream.

Blue Crush

This is one fine way to get your antioxidants, with fresh blueberries and mint—a drink so lush, it's like a great crush, finding yourself immediately coming back for more.

Lemon wedge
Superfine sugar
2 ounces premium vodka
1½ ounce Sweet-and-Sour Syrup (page 31)
¼ cup fresh or thawed frozen blueberries
1 fresh mint leaf

Garnish:
1 small fresh mint sprig

Rub the rim of a chilled cocktail glass with the lemon wedge and rim with sugar (see page 29). In a cocktail shaker, shake the vodka, Sweet-and-Sour Syrup, blueberries, and mint leaf vigorously with ice. Strain carefully into the prepared glass. Garnish with the mint sprig.

Love Potion #9

Like all great love potions, this one is super-potent and will push anyone over the edge into the amour abyss, courtesy of Parfait Amour, that virtual liquid aphrodisiac served in turn-of-the-century Parisian brothels. Prepare yourself for the flavors of violet, vanilla, and orange to kiss your lips.

¼ ounce Parfait Amour (violet liqueur)
1½ ounces orange vodka
½ ounce Cointreau
¼ ounce Chambord
¾ ounce Sweet-and-Sour Syrup (page 31)
1 tablespoon raspberry sorbet

Swirl the Parfait Amour to coat the inside of a chilled cocktail glass. In a cocktail shaker, shake the rest of the ingredients vigorously with ice. Strain into the prepared glass.

Variation:
For a Love Potion #69, add a float of chilled Champagne.

Peartini

The pure essence of fruit is captured in this subtle and fragrant Martini made with ripe pear and pear brandy. This one deserves a great pear brandy such as Clear Creek or Bonny Doon.

1 lemon wedge
Superfine sugar
$1/4$ cup peeled and diced ripe pear
$1/4$ ounce pear brandy or eau-de-vie
2 ounces good-quality vodka
1 ounce Sweet-and-Sour Syrup (page 31)

Rub the rim of a chilled cocktail glass with the lemon wedge and rim with sugar (see page 29). Muddle the pear and pear brandy together in the bottom of a cocktail shaker. Add the vodka and Sweet-and-Sour Syrup. Shake vigorously with ice. Strain carefully into the prepared glass.

Variation:
For a spicy Asian twist, rub the rim of the glass with fresh ginger and dip in sugar, and add a few thin slices of fresh ginger to the ingredients in the shaker.

Strawberry-Basil Martini

When made with homemade strawberry-infused vodka, this is one of those minimalist Martinis that is simply sublime.

2 ounces Strawberry Vodka (page 25)
3 or 4 fresh basil leaves

Garnish:
1 small fresh basil sprig

In a cocktail shaker, shake the vodka and basil leaves vigorously with ice. Strain into a chilled cocktail glass. Garnish with the basil sprig.

Pink Pussycat

This sexy pink potion is cherry-sweet and creamy—purr-fect! for any self-respecting femme fatale or hepcat not afraid to explore his feminine side. The best way to release that great tart cherry flavor is to muddle the morello cherries to make a purée in the bottom of the shaker first, but the expedient method is to simply shake them with the rest of the ingredients.

3 or 4 morello cherries
   or 1 tablespoon cherry preserves
1½ ounces vanilla vodka,
   homemade (see page 20) or commercial
¼ ounce Frangelico
1 ounce half-and-half

Garnish:
1 orange peel spiral

Muddle the cherries in the bottom of a cocktail shaker. Add the remaining ingredients and shake vigorously with ice. Strain into a chilled cocktail glass. Garnish with the orange spiral.

Raspberry Martini

For those raspberry aficionados who love a good Lemon Drop (page 74), this Martini has your name written all over it. If raspberries are not in season, use thawed frozen raspberries, and Chambord will work in a pinch if crème de framboise is unavailable.

1 lemon wedge
Superfine sugar
¼ cup fresh or thawed frozen raspberries
1 ounce Sweet-and-Sour Syrup (page 31)
2 ounces citron vodka
1 ounce crème de framboise

Rub the rim of a chilled cocktail glass with the lemon wedge and rim with sugar (see page 29). Muddle the raspberries and Sweet-and-Sour Syrup together in a cocktail shaker. Add the vodka and crème de framboise and shake vigorously with ice. Strain carefully into the prepared glass.

Variations:
For a frozen version, combine the ingredients in a blender with ½ cup raspberry sorbet, and blend until smooth.

For a Raspberry-Mint Martini, add 2 to 3 fresh mint leaves before shaking.

Suntory Cocktail

Named after the Japanese distillery that produces Midori, this melon-flavored libation is a fabulous summer Martini. Try this recipe using our Quadruple-Citrus Vodka instead of the lemon-flavored citron vodka, for a cocktail with added citrus complexity.

1½ ounces citron vodka,
    or homemade Quadruple-Citrus Vodka (page 24)
1 ounce Midori or other melon liqueur
1 ounce fresh grapefruit juice

Garnish:
1 thin lemon slice

In a cocktail shaker, shake the ingredients vigorously with ice. Strain into a chilled cocktail glass. Float the lemon slice on top.

The Big O

Stylish, effervescent, and sexy in its simplicity, this amazing libation is one erotic ride of a drink, complete with a seductive rim of raspberry purée. You can substitute any puréed fruit your heart desires. Again, we highly recommend a premium vodka for this martini.

4 or 5 fresh raspberries
2 ounces premium vodka
1 to 2 ounces chilled Champagne

In a bowl, muddle the fresh raspberries until mashed to a fine purée. Transfer to a small, shallow bowl. Dip the rim of a chilled cocktail glass in the raspberry purée. Carefully add the vodka without disturbing the prepared rim, and float the Champagne on top.

Far and Away
Vodka Exotica

This chapter is a gathering of our absolute favorite vodka exotica. Shake up a
few of these cocktails from a different
stratosphere for an experience that will
seduce your senses with surprising and
innovative infusions, aromatic liqueurs,
and uncommon ingredients.

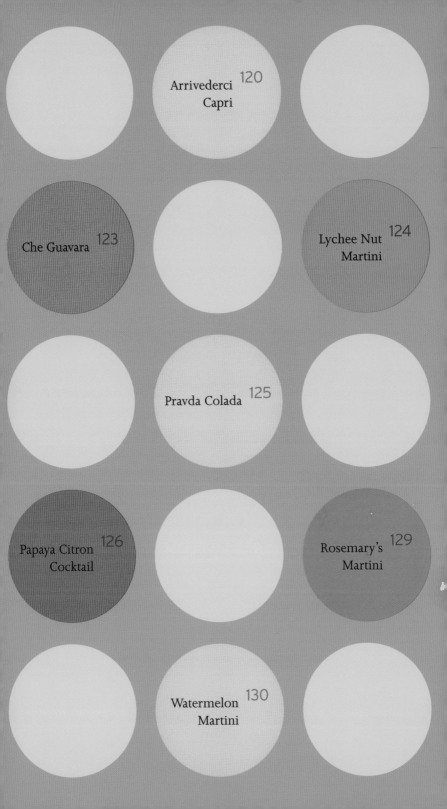

Arrivederci Capri

Much can be said about the origins of a perfectly balanced cocktail. This one began innocently enough at the Bar Tiberio in Capri one hot July afternoon. The inspiration was a large scoop of homemade limone granita doused with lemon vodka. Well, next thing you know the cocktail shaker at Casa Moneta got loaded (it was not the only thing) with Carmelina's homemade limoncello, lemon vodka, and lemon juice fresh from the tree growing outside the kitchen door. The rest, as they say, is history.

1 lemon wedge
Superfine sugar
1½ ounces citron vodka
1 ounce Limoncello liqueur
½ ounce fresh lemon juice

Garnish:
1 thin lemon slice

Rub a chilled cocktail glass with the lemon wedge and rim with sugar (see page 29). In a cocktail shaker, shake the liquid ingredients vigorously with ice. Strain carefully into the prepared glass. Float the lemon slice on top.

Che Guavara

Packed with enough lush flavors to spark a revolution, this is our exotic take on the Cosmopolitan, made with sweet guava nectar (available in well-stocked supermarkets and Hispanic markets) and the nuanced vanilla and orange tones of Tuaca. If you are fortunate enough to find fresh guava in your supermarket, by all means, muddle it in a bowl or process to a purée in a mini food processor and use that in place of the nectar.

1 ½ ounces good-quality vodka
¾ ounce Tuaca
1 ½ ounces guava nectar or fresh guava purée
½ ounce fresh lime juice
Splash of cranberry juice

Garnish:
1 lime peel twist

In a cocktail shaker, shake all the ingredients except the garnish vigorously with ice. Strain into a chilled cocktail glass. Twist the lime peel over the drink and drop it in.

Lychee Nut Martini

Our absolute favorite exotic fruit juice is that of the sweet and fragrant lychee nut: when incorporated into a Martini, it is tropical heaven. This cocktail will send your senses straight to an island idyll. Both lychee juice and liqueur are available in specialty food markets and at international spirit and liqueur Web sites, page 144.

1½ ounces orange vodka
½ ounce lychee nut liqueur
1½ ounces lychee nut juice
1 to 2 ounces chilled club soda

Garnish:
1 lychee nut, sliced in half
1 small, thin orange slice

In a cocktail shaker, shake all the ingredients but the club soda and garnishes vigorously with ice. Strain into a chilled cocktail glass. Float the club soda on top, skewer together the lychee nut and orange slice, and place on the rim.

Pravda Colada

Our answer to the Piña Colada is pushed over the tropical edge with fragrant pineapple-infused vodka for an extra kick of flavor. The classic Colada ingredient is canned, sweetened coconut cream, such as Coco-Loco, sometimes called cream of coconut, and not to be confused with coconut milk. It can be found in the liquor aisle of supermarkets or in liquor stores.

1 $\frac{1}{2}$ ounces Pineapple Vodka (see page 23)
$\frac{1}{2}$ ounce Cointreau
1 $\frac{1}{2}$ ounces pineapple juice
$\frac{1}{2}$ ounce fresh orange juice
$\frac{1}{2}$ ounce fresh lime juice
1 tablespoon coconut cream

Garnish:
1 small fresh pineapple spear

In a cocktail shaker, shake all the ingredients but the garnish vigorously with ice. Strain into a chilled cocktail glass. Garnish with the pineapple spear.

Variation:
For a super-creamy version, add a $\frac{1}{4}$ cup coconut sorbet and combine in a blender until smooth.

Papaya Citron Cocktail

For those who have a passion for tropical fruits and zingy citrus, here's a lush little libation packed with enough exotic flavors to transport your palate to an island paradise. Passion fruit nectar can be found in well-stocked supermarkets or Hispanic markets.

$1\frac{1}{2}$ ounces citron vodka,
    or homemade Quadruple-Citrus Vodka (page 24)
4 ounces passion fruit nectar
1 ounce fresh lime juice
$1\frac{1}{2}$ cups peeled, seeded, and cubed papaya
8 fresh mint leaves

Garnish:
1 thin lime wheel
1 thin papaya slice
1 small fresh mint sprig

Combine all the ingredients but the garnishes in a blender. Blend until smooth. Pour into an ice-filled, large highball glass. Garnish with the lime slice, papaya slice, and mint sprig placed on the rim.

Rosemary's Martini

Herbal Martinis are HOT! The whole herbal-infusion concept is so hip, it has become the cutting edge "must-have" Martini on many cocktail menus. Here is a fantastically refined and aromatically well-balanced expression of this creative movement.

1½ ounces Rosemary Vodka
   (see Lavender Vodka, page 20)
½ ounce Cointreau
¼ ounce fresh lime juice
1 ounce chilled club soda

Garnish:
1 small fresh rosemary sprig

In a cocktail shaker, shake all the ingredients but the club soda and garnish vigorously with ice. Strain into a chilled cocktail glass. Float the club soda on top and garnish with the rosemary sprig.

Watermelon Martini

This Martini is packed with all the super-fresh summer flavors of delicate watermelon and tart citrus. It is guaranteed to immediately conjure a summer picnic in the sunshine with each sip.

¼ cup cubed, seeded watermelon
1½ ounces Watermelon Vodka (page 25)
1 ounce Sweet-and-Sour Syrup (page 31)

Garnish:
1 small fresh mint sprig (optional)
1 small slice of honeydew melon (optional)

Muddle the watermelon in the bottom of a cocktail shaker. Add the vodka and Sweet-and-Sour Syrup, and shake vigorously with ice. Strain into a chilled cocktail glass. Garnish with the mint sprig or a slice of honeydew melon, if desired.

Variation:
To really spark up that picnic-blanket romance, add a float of chilled Champagne.

Siberian Nightcaps

After-Dinner Delectables

These nocturnal cocktails are inspired by moonlight and madness, great for after-dinner late-evening sipping. Whether you are desirous of something creamy and divine or complex and coffee flavored, these decadent libations made with rich liqueurs will soothe the soul, and a few are absolutely ideal for fulfilling those dessert cravings.

Black Martini

Black magic swirls within this minimalist's dream of a midnight martini. A naughty-but-nice rinse of black-hued Opal Nera sambuca whispers its licorice and elderberry tones to a pristine vodka. This cocktail is at its most sublime when made with a premium vodka such as Grey Goose, Ketel One, Belvedere, or Chopin, but to really go to the dark side, try the ink-black-hued Blavod black vodka.

¼ ounce Opal Nera sambuca
2 ounces premium vodka or Blavod black vodka
3 coffee beans

Swirl the sambuca to coat the inside of a chilled cocktail glass. In a cocktail shaker, shake the vodka vigorously with ice. Strain into the prepared glass. Drop in the coffee beans.

Variations:
For a sweet addition, moisten the rim of the glass with sambuca and rim with sugar (see page 29).

For a Berry Black Martini, substitute currant vodka for the regular.

For an unusual presentation dip the rim of the glass in sambuca and then dip into a shallow dish of ground espresso beans.

Euro Night Fever

East meets West in a dance of the potent and sweet. Melding vodka with the herbal, honey tones of Drambuie and rich Metaxa brandy, and blending the mix with vanilla ice cream, chocolate, and splash of club soda for effervescence, makes one dreamy, creamy cocktail. This recipe serves two, but can be multiplied for more.

1½ ounces good-quality vodka
1 ounce Drambuie
1 ounce Metaxa
1 cup vanilla ice cream
¼ cup dark chocolate shavings
2 ounces chilled club soda

Garnish:
Dark chocolate shavings

In a blender, combine the vodka, Drambuie, Metaxa, ice cream, and ¼ cup chocolate shavings with ½ cup crushed ice. Blend until smooth. Add the club soda and blend briefly. Divide the mixture evenly between 2 chilled cocktail glasses. Sprinkle the chocolate shavings garnish on top.

The Siberian Express

This vodka "expresso" cocktail traverses the poles, bringing together vodka from the lands of long winter nights, the Caribbean warmth of spiced rum, a splash of Irish cream, and just enough sweet java flavor and bitter espresso to inspire the limbo over a few snowdrifts.

½ ounce vanilla vodka,
   homemade (see page 20) or commercial
½ ounce Captain Morgan spiced rum
½ ounce Kahlúa
½ ounce Baileys Irish Cream
1 ounce espresso

Garnish:
Pinch of ground cinnamon
3 coffee beans

In a cocktail shaker, shake the liquid ingredients vigorously with ice. Strain into a chilled cocktail glass. Sprinkle with the cinnamon and drop in the coffee beans.

Liquid Raspberry Truffle

Okay, so this may taste more like a rich, high-octane dessert than a cocktail, but when it brings on that state of utter bliss, it will quell the grumblings of even the most extreme cocktail purists.

1 ounce raspberry vodka,
    homemade (see page 24) or commercial
1 ounce Godiva chocolate liqueur
1 ounce Chambord
Splash of heavy cream

Garnish:
Unsweetened cocoa powder or chocolate shavings

In a cocktail shaker, shake the liquid ingredients vigorously with ice. Strain into a chilled cocktail glass. Sprinkle the top with the cocoa powder or chocolate shavings.

Variation:
For a frosty version, combine the ingredients in a blender with ½ cup crushed ice or, for a creamier drink, ½ cup vanilla ice cream, and blend until smooth. Pour into a chilled wineglass.

Dip the rim of a chilled cocktail glass into a shallow bowl of chocolate liqueur, then rim with unsweetened cocoa powder (see page 30) for a more spectacular presentation.

Nutty Ruskei

Actually, the Russians do think we're nutty for wanting to ever sully good vodka with the addition of *anything*, but one sip of this heady combination of hazelnut and coffee flavors may convert those who can't seem to get past even the basic Black Russian.

1 ½ ounces good-quality vodka
½ ounce Kahlúa or Tia Maria
¼ ounce Frangelico

Garnish:
1 lemon peel twist

In a cocktail shaker, shake the liquid ingredients vigorously with ice. Strain into an ice-filled old-fashioned glass. Twist the lemon peel over the drink and drop it in.

Variation:
For a Nutty White Ruskei, add 1 ounce heavy cream, skip the lemon twist, and dust the top with a pinch of ground nutmeg or cinnamon.

White Chocolate Dream

Though it may not seem possible, this sublime cocktail takes the Chocolate Martini up to another level, a high-flying white cloud of a drink.

Powdered sugar
2 ounces good-quality vodka
1 ounce Godiva white chocolate liqueur

Garnish:
1 orange peel twist
White chocolate truffle

Moisten the rim of a chilled cocktail glass with white chocolate liqueur and rim with powdered sugar (see page 29).
In a cocktail shaker, shake the liquid ingredients vigorously with ice. Strain into the prepared glass. Twist the orange peel over the drink and drop it in. Garnish with the truffle.

Variation:
For those who cannot get enough of the orange-chocolate combo, moisten the rim with an orange wedge before dipping in the powdered sugar, and add ½ ounce Tuaca.

Index

Internet Spirits and Liqueurs Web Sites

If you are looking for a particular vodka or the exotic and seemingly unobtainable liquors and liqueurs you are unable to get at your local liquor store, such as lychee liqueur, you can always find them available on the Web.

Here is our list of the best liquor store Web sites that will ship to your door:

- wallywine.com
  Has a great selection of liquor and exotic liqueurs.

- wineglobe.com
  A huge selection of premium vodkas and flavored vodkas as well as great liqueur selection.

- internetwinesandspirits.com
  A great selection of ultra-premium and flavored vodkas, along with a "favorite picks" critique.

- konawinemarket.com
  Offers a large selection of hard to find liqueurs and spirits.

Liquid Measurements

Bar spoon	½ ounce
1 teaspoon	⅙ ounce
1 tablespoon	½ ounce
2 tablespoons (pony)	1 ounce
3 tablespoons (jigger)	1½ ounces
¼ cup	2 ounces
⅓ cup	3 ounces
½ cup	4 ounces
⅔ cup	5 ounces
¾ cup	6 ounces
1 cup	8 ounces
1 pint	16 ounces
1 quart	32 ounces
750 ml bottle	25.4 ounces
1 liter bottle	33.8 ounces
1 medium lemon	3 tablespoons juice
1 medium lime	2 tablespoons juice
1 medium orange	⅓ cup juice